SO-DZN-717

Get Ready!

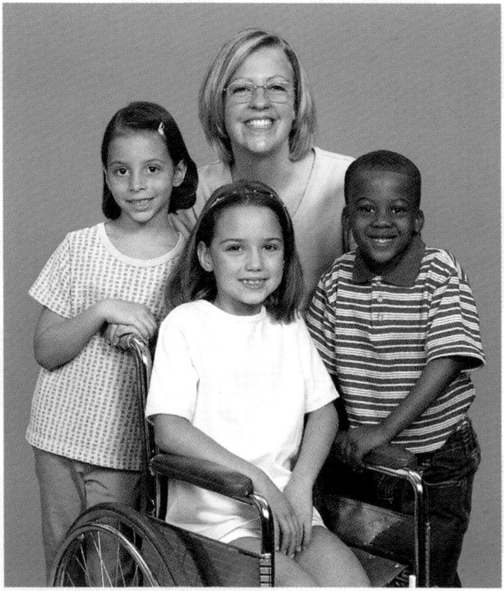

Nina Tsang

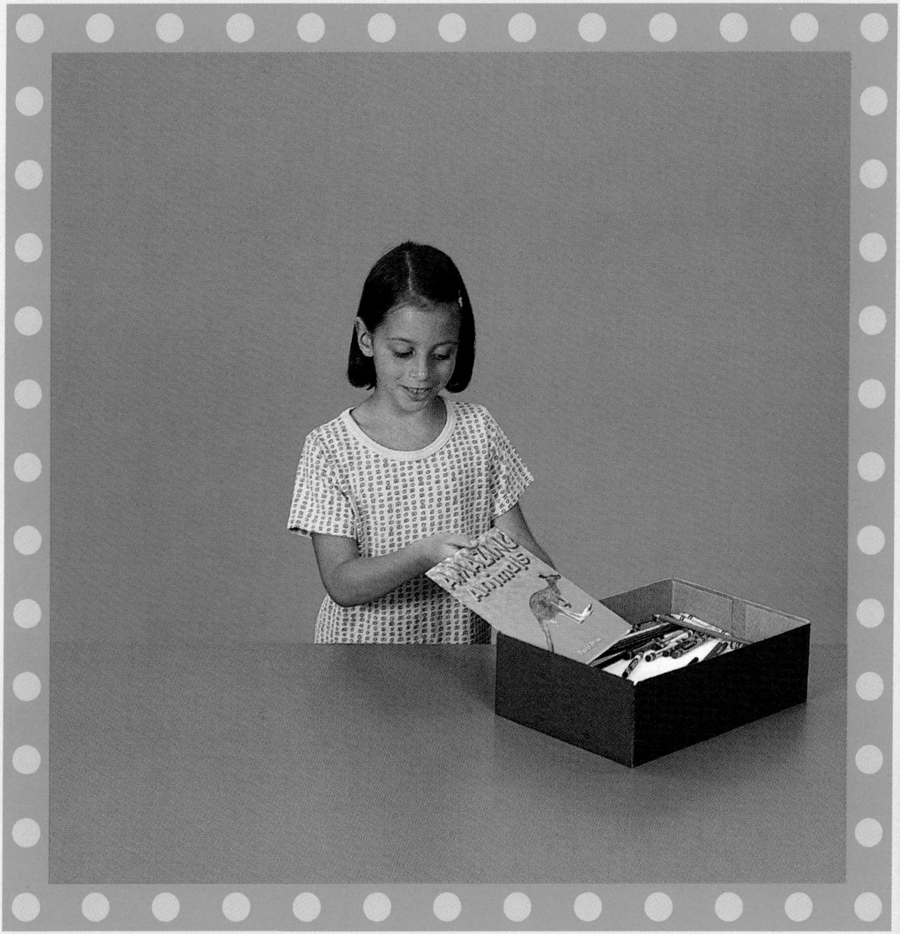

Get your book.

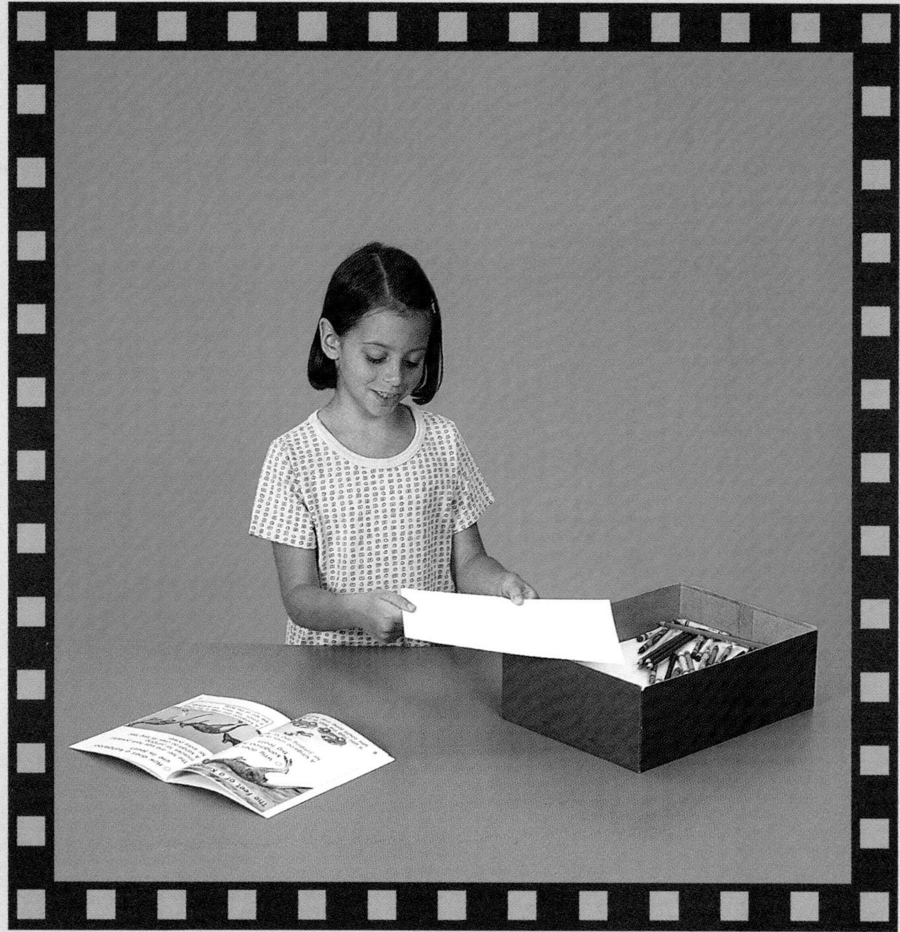

Get your paper.

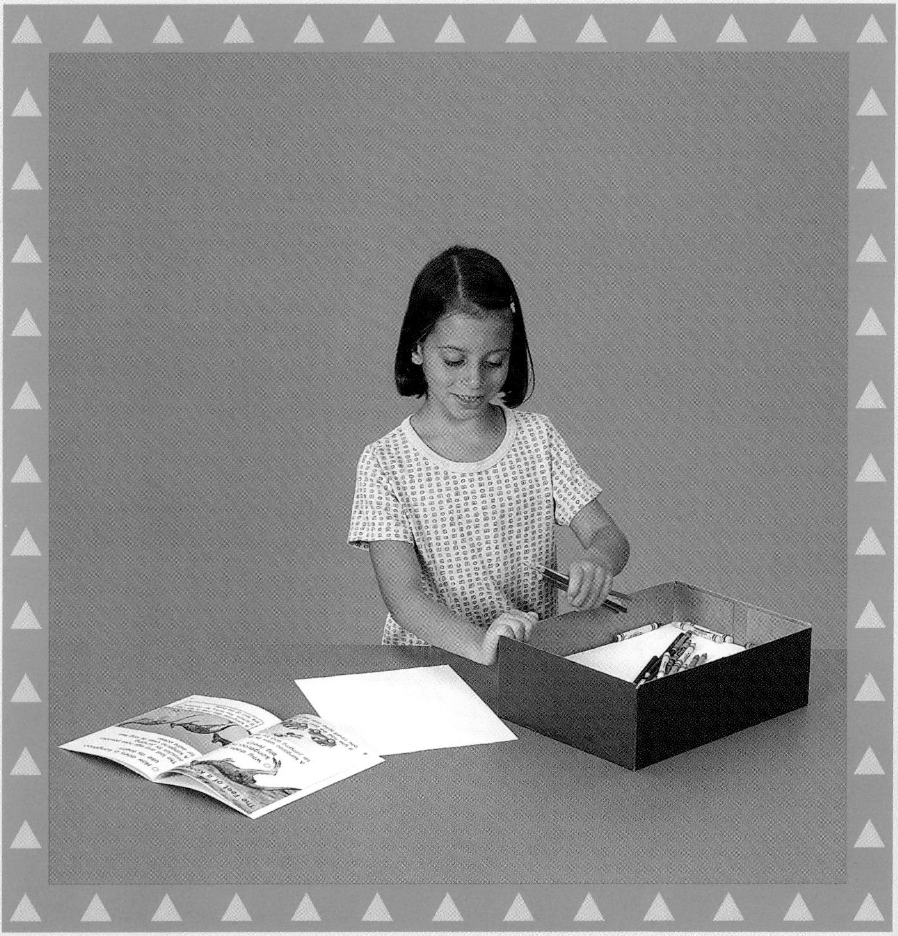

Get your pencils.

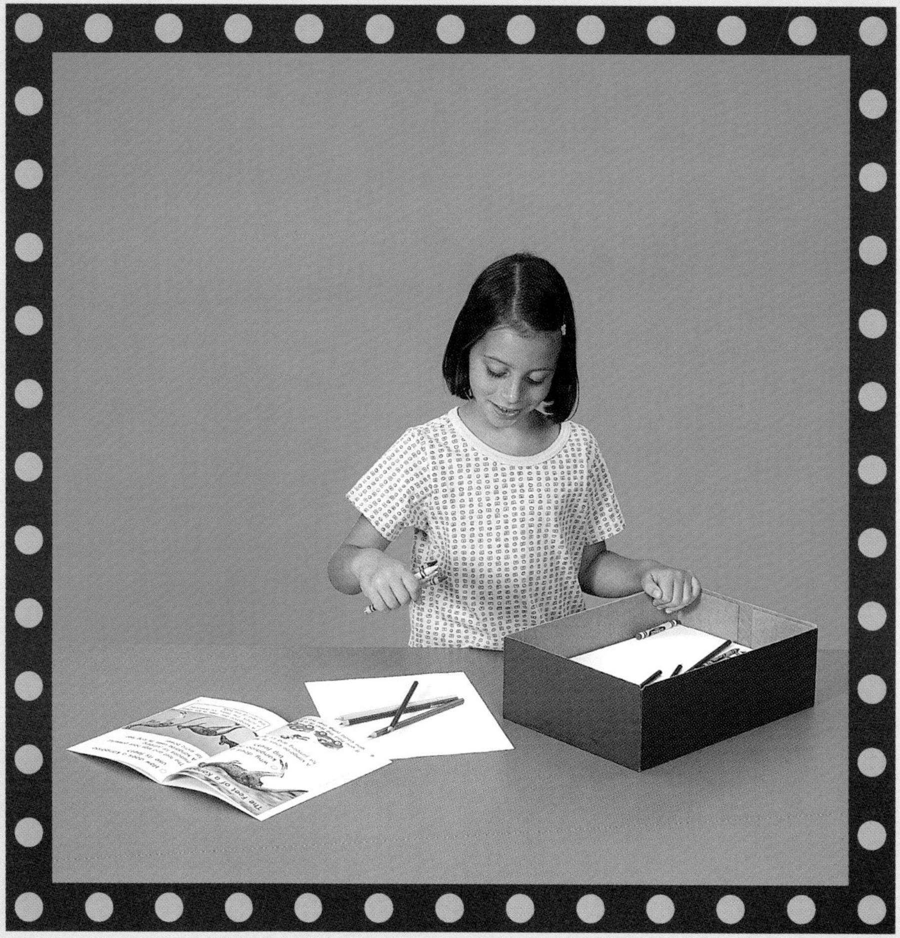

Get your crayons.

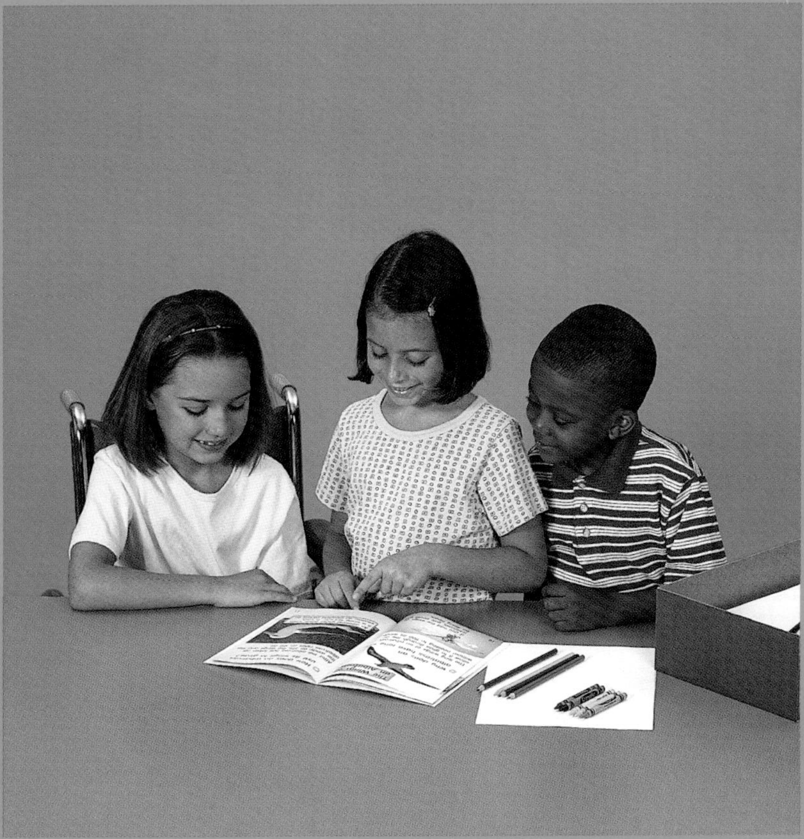

Get your friends.

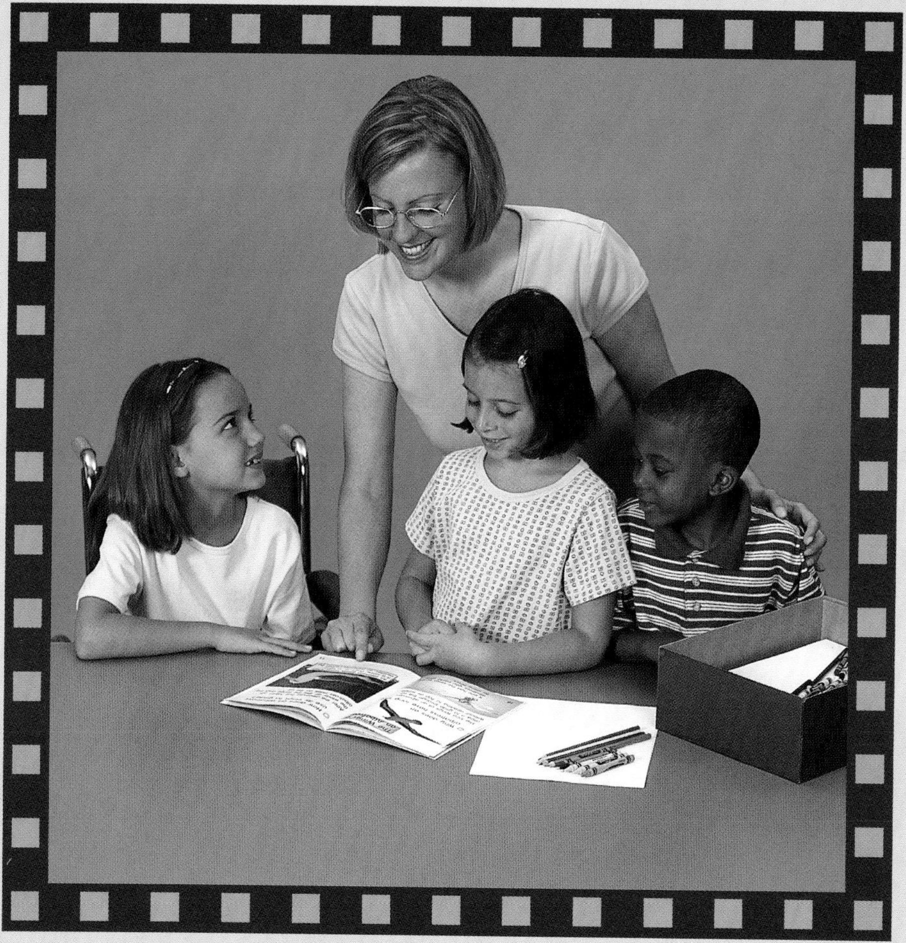

Get your teacher.

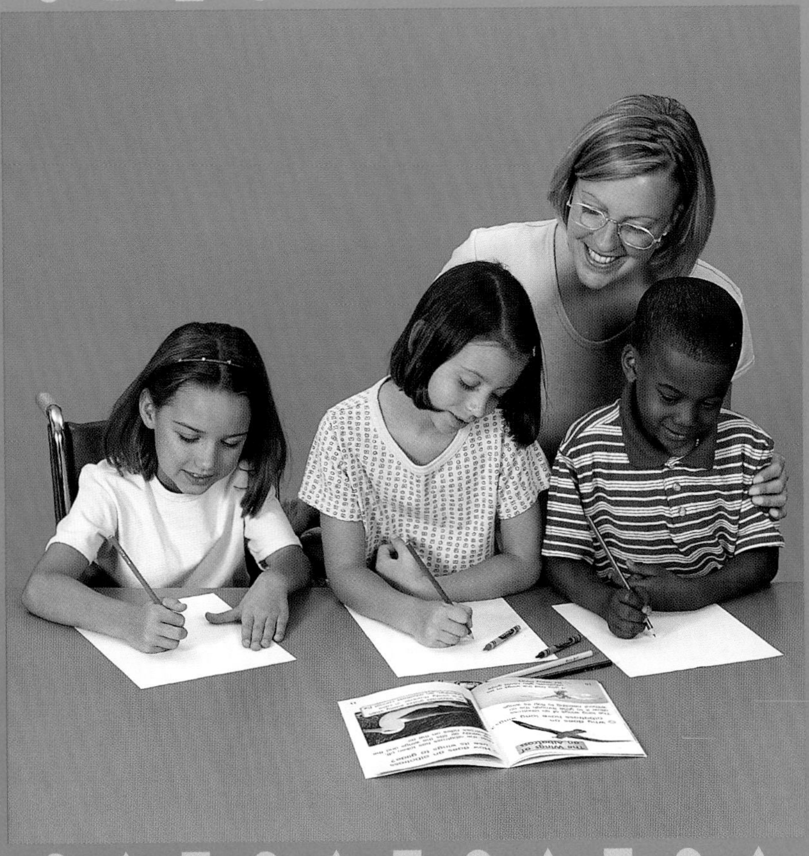

Now you are ready!